DIANA WOLFE

Paid to Persuade

A Guide to Sales Slants

First published by Sun City Art Press 2020

Copyright © 2020 by Diana Wolfe

All rights reserved. No part of this publication may be reproduced, stored or transmitted in any form or by any means, electronic, mechanical, photocopying, recording, scanning, or otherwise without written permission from the publisher. It is illegal to copy this book, post it to a website, or distribute it by any other means without permission.

Designations used by companies to distinguish their products are often claimed as trademarks. All brand names and product names used in this book and on its cover are trade names, service marks, trademarks and registered trademarks of their respective owners. The publishers and the book are not associated with any product or vendor mentioned in this book. None of the companies referenced within the book have endorsed the book.

First edition

Cover art by "Book Cover Design by ebooklaunch.com"

This book was professionally typeset on Reedsy. Find out more at reedsy.com

To my mother, Pauline Wolfe, teacher of excellence, and to my grandfather, George W. Harmon, salesman extraordinaire and master of self-reinvention.

Contents

1	Acknowledgements	1
2	The Greatest Profession on Earth	2
3	Plan to Double Your Income	5
4	Sell to Vanity	11
5	The Professional Salesperson's Creed	14
6	Sales Slants	17
7	Mastery Principles of Selling	19
8	Sales Talk Examples	21
9	Retail Selling Talk	30
10	Sales Talk Starters	36
11	Daily Affirmations	43
12	In Closing	45
13	Bibliography	46
14	Conclusion	48
	Epilogue	49
	About the Author	50

1

Acknowledgements

To everyone who adventures forth, sure that a new opportunity is right around the corner. To those who pick themselves up in the face of change and keep on loving the people they find in every nook and corner of the world. You are the greatest, you are the rock stars, you are the real MVPs.

2

The Greatest Profession on Earth

Courage is resistance to fear, mastery of fear, not absence of fear.

—Mark Twain

Rest assured that selling is a professional job, and just as much of one as being a physician. What a physician is to public health and healing, and an engineer is to building, the salesperson is to business.

Salespeople perform one of the most valuable functions in society. A great salesperson helps people evaluate market offers for the money they spend. A great salesperson must know as much about the likes, dislikes and motivations of people as any psychiatrist.

Professional salespeople have the enviable chance to give their clients professional services and expertise. Selling is a professional job, whether you're working for yourself or for someone else. This book is about how to be a professional instead of an amateur.

Selling is the greatest profession on earth! Be proud, and take a bow. Sure your sales can run higher one month, and lower the next. There is always a new day around the corner. One of the most dangerous things a salesperson can do is get into a rut during a low month. Sure, it is easy to do. The main difference in a rut and a grave is how deep. Right? In sales, you must know your product or service thoroughly. Take the time to study up, ask questions, read and review materials until you know them backwards and forwards. You must study and review over and over. A great salesperson knows more about the product or service he or she is selling than the buyer. What seems old to the salesperson may be new to the buyer. You, as the salesperson, must be aware of how to classify your prospective buyer. Speaking the language of your prospect is essential. If you can find out the buyer's hobby, then it gives you something to connect through and meet him or her on familiar territory.

Keep your chin up! Remember, there is no substitute for hard work and determination. Make your sales plan and work it. Fear is the enemy of good salesmanship. Check your posture and stand up straight. You are a professional and just as good as anyone else, no matter where you started out.

If you have anxiety about your sales plan, change it before you proceed further. Your sales plan cannot work the same way for every prospect, so your plan needs the right tools to adapt to the needs of the kind of prospects you will encounter. A pro always needs the right tools at hand. You have to be mature and have good common sense to be able to judge the types of people you are dealing with and know how to work with them. This kind of common sense is way more valuable than a master's or bachelor's degree.

3

Plan to Double Your Income

The starting point of all achievement is DESIRE. Keep this constantly in mind. Weak desire brings weak results, just as a small fire makes a small amount of heat.

— Napoleon Hill

You are the captain of your own ship. As captain, you are responsible for your own losses and failures. I know that is hard to hear at times. However, facing this truth always frees you up to sail your way around the world with a surer path. You are not responsible for the amount of intelligence you started out with in life, but you are responsible for what you make of the intelligence you have got!

Plan your work and work your plan. When you get to the point where you know what your prospective buyer wants and what he or she has in mind, you can begin to sell that buyer. Right up until that point, you are only talking. Conversations will not put cash in the bank, but they start you in the right direction.

Top salespeople will keep the habit of working quickly to find out one important thing. **Top salespeople find out what the prospect is thinking about.** Price, features, and style are just some kindling to spark a sale. There are loads of important facts that questions can nurture into conversations leading in the direction of a sale. When you have these facts, you are ready to go to work. Trying to sell without knowing what your prospective buyer is thinking about leaves you in the dark.

Take the direct route to find territory either in person or online to find prospects who are willing to buy. Every megastar salesperson wants to know, in real time, who is in their territory right now and ready to buy?

Times keep changing with the rapidly accelerating pace of technology. Your working map of territories needs to keep changing also. Prospects may be harder to find in old places, but do keep searching out all viable avenues—in person, social media, websites, telephone, and mail. Ask friends and acquaintances for names. There are people out there ready to buy, but unless you search them out, they are not buying from you.

Selling is telling. How is your sales presentation, and website FAQ section? Do you know all the answers to your prospect's questions? You cannot guess. You must know. No professional makes guesses. The expert must know!

Often, it does not necessarily take anything inventive, new or special to make more sales. This should be an encouragement. Many excellent salespersons will increase sales by doing what they have always done to make sales, but more of it, and they will increase their volume of sales. When you play the numbers game, you may find more people along the way who are not really interested in your product or service. Discard these prospects. Go out after new prospects, and focus on the ones you know are able to buy from you. You must have prospects to make sales. Our job in selling is to keep a constant stream of good prospects. It helps to put yourself in a target rich environment. Make a list of good potential environments and list of sales prospects. Our prospect list is one of the first places that more concentrated efforts will show direct results in increased sales.

After you have identified prospects, be sure you have the right approach. Your manner of approaching someone is extremely important. **The first impression people make of you lasts forever.** Many people will size you up in the first 30 seconds. The same principle goes for your social media. A person will either like you or not. You must gain the person's trust and confidence. There is more than one way to accomplish this. Sincerity is one great way. You must love people! If you like and love the people you meet, then it isn't hard to be sincere with them. Always try to be neutral. Never wear the "I am all that and a bag of chips" conveying a bragging air or try to come across as you are the boss and superior. That turns people off quick. Dominate the situation, steer the interaction but like a professional. Be smooth, not smug.

Great salespeople should never lose sight of the idea that the goal is to make prospects see things the salesperson's way. The concept of being paid to persuade is using the art of rhetoric, which is verbal and written words, to influence people to agree with your point of view.

The business community draws a sharp distinction between salespeople and clerks. A clerk's job is to wait on customers, ring up their purchases, accept their money and wrap up and bag their purchases. A clerk may offer an online loyalty or discount program with a card also. A salesperson's job is to sell the prospect by meeting a need that the prospect did not even know he or she had. The salesperson must make the customer realize the merits of the product or service are so valuable that he or she will pay the price to get that **particular** product or service. A great salesperson was able to sell him or herself to their firm, and the same logic will sell the prospect. Human beings work this way the world over. A big mistake is assuming the prospect knows as much about a product or service as the salesperson does. If that were true, then with a quality product or service, nobody would need to actually sell it.

Power Map to Double your Income

1. Prepare all details of any morning phone calls, emails, or social media posts the evening before.
2. Attend to all personal business—showering, grooming, breakfast, personal texts, errands—before 8:00 am.
3. Start working by 8:00 am.
4. Attend any morning meeting or conference calls you may have when house rules require it.
5. Get your sales work underway by 8:15 am. Make any calls or send any texts, emails or social media posts you planned the night before.
6. Make five or more calls, texts or emails to satisfied owners of your product or service, with a definite message in mind. Ask each person this question: "Who can you recommend that should own one of our products or services? Please give me a testimonial note, email, letter, or good online

review."
7. Make five or more calls, or texts to the live prospects of your personal list.
8. Make five or more straight cold canvass calls in any one territory you physically work, preferably in a zone or building
9. Demonstrate your product or service to no less than five prospects daily if you are working in person.
10. Write ten emails daily, preferably from a selected list of people. Include language about prices, value and the many advantages of your product or service. Be sure to provide all of your contact details, phone, email, website and social media.
11. Write ten emails to prospects once per week recommending any product or service you feel has sales appeal to that prospect.
12. If you have a product or service that can be demonstrated, ask five people every day for the privilege of demonstrating.
13. Make some form of personal acknowledgement for every sale, either by email, letter, personal call or text.
14. Maintain a close, friendly follow up with each new owner after a sale is made. Inquire as the owner's satisfaction with the product or service and ask for prospects.
15. Use a personal selling card on which is printed your name, all contact information, and information about price, features and terms for your product or service.

So, there you have the plan! Here is the challenge: do you have the guts and stamina to carry it out?

Only you can determine that. You should really find out. Forge ahead and live your life to your own satisfaction with the results of your increased profits.

Selling like a professional is the finest, most rewarding and fruitful career that any person may pursue. Put your heart and soul into it, and many rewards will follow. You are not just working a job. You are an artist and a scientist. Sure, some people may have looked upon you as an unnecessary person. However, you, the sales professional, are one of the most needed persons on this planet earth. Without you, most industries and businesses would stop, wither and die off, deprived of cash flow in the right direction. Sales requires a data driven as well as a human approach. You must adapt and meet the needs of every personality. You have your own ups and downs to manage like everyone else, but you stay determined and motivated. If you learn to like the great things about people, they will stay interesting to you. Then, they will like you in return and will want to do business with you also.

Sales must stay flexible and adapt to people. Selling must persuade and encourage people. Selling can be done by anyone with the right mental outlook. Your mind is the greatest part of your body. Use it to succeed and help others!

4

Sell to Vanity

When dealing with people, remember you are not dealing with creatures of logic, but with creatures bristling with prejudice and motivated by pride and vanity.

— Dale Carnegie, How to Win Friends and Influence People

Vanity is a personal characteristic that is present in each and every person to varying degrees. You can harness the vanity of prospective buyers. Bright colors, graceful lines, and a sense of beauty appeal to a prospect. A good salesperson pitches to this very human quality. I believe that a salesperson passes up a good bet when he or she fails to realize that all people are a little bit vain. At the right time, a good salesperson may pay a compliment to the prospect. Skillfully playing on the prospect's vanity can be a great help in closing many a sale. Here is an example using car sales:

One day one of our salesmen told me how Mr. and Mrs. Garcia needed a new BMW sedan. In spite of all his efforts, he still felt like he was going to lose out to the competition at another car dealer. He asked me to go talk to Mr. and Mrs. Garcia and try to move the sale.

When I called her, I said, "Mrs. Garcia, I don't believe you have been into our store. If you will be kind enough to come in tonight, we have a pleasant surprise for you—and the salesman will get extra credit for your visit."

She answered, "Mr. Green, we are buying another make of car, and we hate to take up your time. However, if it will help the salesman any, we will come in at 7:15 pm."

When Mr. and Mrs. Garcia came to the salesroom that evening, I showed them our complete new line of cars. Once more, Mrs. Garcia said was sorry she could not buy that BMW—but they felt obligated to the competitive salesperson because she had been letting them drive her demonstrator for four days.

I replied, "I promised you a surprise, so please come this way," and took them over to a fully equipped, deluxe, BMW four door sedan painted blue. Opening the door, I asked Mrs. Garcia to get in and I adjusted the seat for her. Then I said, "Now, do you admire beautiful pictures? Well, I'm going to show you what I think is a beautiful picture."

Next, I quickly snapped her picture with my phone, held it so she could see herself and exclaimed, "Now, there is a beautiful picture—a beautiful lady and a beautiful car! The color of the car just suits her; don't you think so Mr. Garcia?"

He said, "Yes, I'll have to admit it."

For the next 30 minutes, I preached BMW. We went for a ride in the car, and during the demonstration I said, "Mrs. Garcia, this beautiful blue BMW is the only one of these in town right now, and we won't be able to keep it for long. If you order it now, I can deliver it to you tonight."

She did that very thing, and Mrs. Garcia took the competitor's demonstrator car back to the showroom that very night.

I believe a salesperson passes up a good bet when he or she fails to realize that all people are a little bit vain. He or she should, at the right time, pay the prospect a compliment. No matter how they are, find something!

Skillfully playing on the prospect's ego and vanity can be of great help in closing many a sale!

Be proud that your hard work is not in vain. Feel proud that it has cost, and that the fruits of your work are worth every atom of the price. Think of your tasks like a medical doctor does. A doctor's battles are won because of necessary plans and preparation. Try to sell yourself on your plan first, and then **work** the plan.

Salespeople perform one of the most valuable services in modern society. A great salesperson helps people obtain the fullest value of the money they spend. A salesperson has to know much about people's likes and dislikes—their needs and desires—as much as any other professional who makes a living dealing with people.

5

The Professional Salesperson's Creed

Our greatest weakness lies in giving up. The most certain way to succeed is always to try just one more time.

—Thomas Edison

My Creed

- I believe in the products and services I am selling, in the firm I am working for, and in my ability to get results.
- I believe that honest products and services can be sold to honest people through honest methods.
- I believe in working, not waiting, in laughing, not crying, in boosting, not knocking, and in the pleasure of selling.
- I believe a person gets what he or she goes after, that

one order today is worth two orders tomorrow, and that no person is down and out until they have lost faith in themselves.
- I believe in today and the work I am doing, in tomorrow and the work I hope to do, and in the sure reward which the future holds.
- I believe in courtesy, in kindness, in generosity, in good cheer, in friendship and honest competition.
- I believe there is an order out there somewhere for every person ready to take one.
- I believe I am ready right this minute.

The Real Salesperson

- One who has a steady nerve, a steady eye, and a steady heart.
- One who understands people and makes him or herself useful.
- One who turns up with a smile and still smiles when things turn down.
- One who tries to outthink the buyer rather than outthink the boss.
- One who is silent when he or she has nothing to say, and also silent when the buyer has something to say.
- One who takes a firm interest in the **firm's** interest.
- One who wins respect by being respectful.
- One who keeps his or her word, his or her temper, and his or her friends.
- One who has the power to persuade.

When selling, be sure to use common sense salesmanship, and play up the prospects special interests, as well as your product or service's style, appearance, handling and benefits.

6

Sales Slants

The way to get started is to quit talking and begin doing.

—Walt Disney

- People will never be persuaded unless you expose yourself to them. Go ahead and do the math. Divide the number of hours you put into your work by the numbers of hours spent in the field or online interacting with your sales prospects. This will show you the real time percentage of your efficiencies.
- Please do something. In case you were wondering, it is better to do something wrong than not to try to do it at all.
- We all make mistakes. Go ahead and look at yours. Don't turn away, just profit from them instead. Scan and analyze your artist's canvas, search your days' worth of work so you

can find whatever went wrong and correct it.
- Organize yourself and then organize your physical territory, and online presence.
- Do not expect somebody else to rescue you by doing your work for you.
- Do not take up with an organization where everyone is a boss and nobody is a worker bee.
- The sale is the shortest distance it takes to get between two points, so he who rambles is lost in the weeds.

7

Mastery Principles of Selling

The value of a man should be seen in what he gives and not in what he is able to receive.

—Albert Einstein

- Keep your airtime to 40 percent or less. Don't do more than your share of the talking.
- Never interrupt your prospect.
- Do not unconsciously get defensive and slip into debating or arguing.
- Ask for the prospect's objections to the sale, if there are any.
- Everybody has one big issue. Be on the lookout to discover it. Stick to the big issue, and do not allow your prospect to get sidetracked.
- Get the attention of your prospect and hold it.
- Find out if your prospect has any money to spend.

- Learn how much your prospect is earning.
- Show your prospect that your product or service will save him or her money.
- Talk about the substantial customers you have now, and have had in the past.
- Do not be too anxious. Encourage the prospect to talk.
- Remind your prospect that there are many people who already own your product or service or want to.
- Listen to your prospect's objections, then overcome them.
- Watch for a favorable moment to close the sale.
- Create the belief and feeling that the prospect—not you—will be the one to profit from the sale.
- No person has lost all who has not lost faith in themselves.

8

Sales Talk Examples

I had so many people try to talk me out of starting a rocket company, it was crazy.

—Elon Musk

The first essential quality of a great salesperson is to know your goods or services. Every salesperson reading this book is going to call between two and twelve prospects tomorrow. Some people are going to make a sale, some people are not and they are not going to understand why. There are no set rules to selling products or services. If there were, all a salesperson would have to do would be to memorize the rules and he or she would be a world beater. However, there are certain general principles of selling which must be observed if you expect to make much of a productive sales record. Some of these principles are simple and can be read and digested, then worked into your daily routine. This will result in more sales.

Many a sale has been lost in the first ten seconds that the salesperson talks to the prospect. Why is that? Well, if the person doesn't know the salesperson, it is during this period that the person decides whether he or she likes the salesperson personally. If the prospect doesn't like you, you're sunk because all the knowledge and all the high powered salesmanship in the world won't do you any good. **The approach, then, is all important.**

There are many ways of approaching a person, but one of the best ways is to start the conversation by talking about something the prospect is interested in. Whether it's horses, golf, slab cars, survival skills, fashion, babies or traveling to Peru, whatever it is, start talking about the prospect's interests. You'll get the person's attention, and the chances are you'll make a favorable impression, and that is important in selling.

As soon as you can, transfer the prospect's attention from these things and yourself to the product or service you want to sell.

There are few prospects in these days of stiff competition and widespread advertising that have made up their minds as to what product or service to buy when they get ready for it. Every website, blog, social media feed, email, newspaper, radio and magazine and every salesperson tells the prospect that he or she would be making a grave mistake by buying any product or service but his or hers. In the face of this bewildering array of extravagant statements, it is no wonder that the prospect hesitates to plunk down hard-earned money for any particular product or service.

Think of it this way. You know you have the best buy, but the prospect doesn't, and your job is to prove that you have the best value that will give more for the money for that service or greater satisfaction than any other product or service he or she can buy. After doing that—get his or her order!

After you have obtained the prospect's confidence, then you should ask him or her a question—a question that is used by thousands of salespeople all over the world, whether it's for selling computers, smart phones, software, soap, robots, hardware, cars, or guitars. All successful salespeople in all lines tailor the same question to suit their product or service. This question is called "the approach" and it is used to get your prospect to say yes right off the bat. Here is an ideal approach that you should memorize:

"Mr. Jones, if I can prove to you that this Toyota automobile can give you more comfortable and satisfactory service, at less cost than any other car, you'd be interested in knowing it wouldn't you?"

Nine prospects out of ten will say **yes**, and when they do, they have invited you to go ahead and prove the superiority of your product or service and have already agreed to listen.

The tenth person will try to put you off and get rid of you. Why? This prospect is afraid that if he or she lets you go ahead, you'll sell him or her. Therefore, you should stick to this person like glue if you can, without getting him or her peeved at you, in an endeavor to make the prospect listen to what you have to say. The favorite stalls of most of these kinds of prospects are "I'm too busy," "I haven't got time," "See me some other time about it," "I'll see you later," "I'll drop into the place next week and see you," and so forth like that.

Try this comeback:

"Mr. Jones, I know you're busy. I am too, but my proposition is either a good thing, or it isn't, and it is either to your

advantage, or it isn't; hence, I am willing to put a little of my time against a little of yours, and tell you about it. That's fair enough isn't it?"

The chances are the prospect will say "Yeah, I guess so." Then is when you can open up with your sales talk. It is a great idea to try and arouse the prospect's curiosity at this point. A successful salesperson uses a line such as the following to get and hold the prospect's interest:

Mr. Jones, I believe I know what you are going to expect in the car you buy. You're going to expect four things:

You want a good-looking and easy-riding car. Notice the full stream lines from front to back—the graceful effect of the window moldings, the low rakish top with the military style visor. Come around to the front. You've seen the front end of the Honda, well the radiator and headlight arrangement is almost identical, only smaller of course; in fact, the new Toyota bodies and lines are very similar to the fashionable body designs of the Lexus, BMW and other fine body builders and designers. In addition, you have a choice of fifteen beautiful colors, something unusual in a lower priced car.

As for easy riding, you have four high quality shock absorbers—the best that money can buy anywhere—that make this car ride like a baby carriage. I'll prove that to you in a minute. Look under here at the clearance between the axle and the ground. You have more than on any other car on the market, making it easier to go over mud holes and over high centers without sticking.

The second thing you want is a car with plenty of power, pep and speed, and yet a safe car to drive. The car has a great cooling system, and our ignition system is so waterproof you can drive this car in the rain with the hood off and it won't

drown out. *Talk some more about all the specifications and attributes here.* More speed than this is dangerous, unless provision has been made to make the car absolutely safe. We believe the safety principle has been carried out to the limit in the new Toyota car. *Elaborate further on safety features here.*

A recent case illustrating these safety features occurred in Colorado the other day. A man driving a Toyota through the mountains tried to change the music on his phone via Spotify while rounding a curve. He went off a bank, and the car turned three complete somersaults down the hill landing right side up—driver unhurt and the car practically unscratched. Not even glass broken.

The third thing you want is a strong company and manufacturer backing the product you buy, and a reliable team to give you service. *Talk here about the values of your company and how well they are visibly demonstrated.* After that, say, "I believe you have confidence in the firm and our sincere desire to give you the very best service. Our interest does not stop after you buy from us. We want you to be a booster for our products and for our service. We have a large stock of parts. We have invested in modern service operations designed to deliver quick service at minimal cost to you, and you'll find we have a professionally trained service crew who will take a personal interest in the performance of the product you purchased. Our place is always kept clean and presentable, so the customers can walk through easily. We find that this is a good business practice as our customers like it."

The fourth thing you want is long, trouble-free service for a product at the least cost to you, and then, finally, when you get ready to replace or upgrade it, you have received the full value of it. Isn't that right? *Talk here about how many people nation or world-wide have purchased the product.*

"How do you wish to pay for the car, Mr. Jones?" "Cash, or would you prefer the time payment plan? If he says "cash" or "the time payment plan," either one, hand him a pencil or the laptop computer to sign the order—which you have already made out in advance with his type product inserted and everything filled in except his name.

The salesperson must keep in mind that many a prospect has been talked into buying a product and then talked right back out of it by the salesperson who didn't have the nerve enough to stop his or her sales talk at the right place, and give the prospect an opportunity to sign on the dotted line. It doesn't matter where you are in your sales talk—if you sense your prospect has begun to make up his or her mind, drag out your order paperwork or online form, then tell him or her to write a signature on the lower right hand line. The records show that the most successful salespeople in the country are the ones who keep asking the prospect to sign the order. For instance, a great salesperson makes six points with a prospect, and after each point he hands the prospect a pencil and asks him or her to write his or her name on the order. The sixth time the prospect orders the stuff. This is a great way to be the top performer on a sales team.

I know many of you will follow up after talking with your prospect by asking the prospect for the sale, but don't know just how to get to the matter in a diplomatic and graceful way. One of the best strategies that top salespeople use every day is to try and get the prospect's decision on a minor point. Give the prospect two favorable choices. Ask questions about these two choices, the answer to either of which will mean he or she has bought your product or service. For example, "Which payment plan would be more satisfying to you—the cash or the time payment plan?" If your prospect answers this question and says "Cash," then lay down the order for him to sign. By this question you are backing the prospect into a corner, and he will have to make an offer to escape.

Maybe you have two colors. Ask him, "Do you want the blue or the brown one, Mr. Jakobs?" The answer is a sale, unless he hedges, and hedging means loads of extra effort. Many a sale throughout history has been closed this way. If your product has an accessory already attached to it, then get your prospect to agree on a minor point by asking if he or she wants that particular accessory that is already fastened onto the product. If the prospect says "No, I don't want that," then say, "Alright, I will call the service department and have that taken off for you." Then, call service and have them take the accessory off for that particular product, again dragging out your laptop or order pad, and telling your prospect to write his name and you will get the product ready for him. IF the prospect says "Yes" to your question, say, "All right—fine!" and then call the service department and tell them to get the product ready for Mr. Jakobs and consider the matter a sale until and unless he balks. If he does, talk about the product from another angle. Tell him how you can handle some aspect in a different way than what he already knew about.

Let me tell you right here that the best way to upsell extra accessories is in groups, and when writing up an order, tell the prospect that he or she can get all the accessories for a lump sum of so much. He may tell you to write it up that way. If the prospect balks, then you still have an opportunity to sell him or her individual items. This process is called bundling, and it works whether you are a merchant seller peddling handmade crafts on Amazon or Etsy, or selling luxury cars such as a BMW.

IF after all your efforts he still holds out, then pull out your ace in the hole—<u>the demonstration</u>.

Be sure your demonstration product is in perfect condition, and show the prospect its great features and efficiency. Point out all the good features by actual demonstration. Ask him if he won't slide his hand over and touch the product too. This is the most successful method to get your prospect to test the product.

When you are finished demonstrating, assume he is going to buy the product and ask him to sign.

Suppose the prospect says, "How soon can you deliver XY Super Gadget to me?" What would you say? Let me tell you of an experience that happened in Atlanta last week. The salesman, a splendid fellow and enthusiastic talker, had his prospect work up fine. He went right down the line with him, demonstrated the product, and as I was walking past, I heard the prospect ask him, "How soon can you deliver the product?"

The salesman came back right away like a flash and said, "Right away Mr. Wilson." What do you suppose Mr. Wilson said?

Here's what he said, "Well, there's no hurry. I'll think it over and see you next week." He shook hands with the salesman and walked out of the place. The salesman lost a sale that he would have been able to make money over. What was wrong in that answer? The psychology of the thing was that the salesman had the prospect worked up to the point of asking about the delivery of the product, but the prospect unwittingly and unwillingly, by the nature of his question and the salesman's answer, changed the one of the <u>delivery date</u>—an entirely irrelevant matter when it comes to closing the sale. The salesman's answer left the case wide open for the prospect to put off buying with an old excuse of not being in a hurry about buying, and the salesman didn't have a persuasive comeback.

Now, what should the salesman have said when the prospect asked, "How soon can you deliver the car?" he should have answered this question by asking the prospect another, namely, "How soon do you want it?" or "When do you have to have it?" This then puts the prospect back on the defensive, and he has to give the salesperson an answer. Here, the answer is the sale of the product and the delivery date ALL IN ONE, as determined by the prospect and not the salesperson.

Remember to keep your prospect on the defensive, always.

9

Retail Selling Talk

Courage is what it takes to stand up and speak; courage is also what it takes to sit down and listen.

—Winston Churchill.

In retail selling especially, you really have to mind your manners, and to be successful you really need a lot of courage and guts. The good news is that anybody can learn to have courage. Courage is acting in the face of fear, not acting without fear.

Of all the thousands of excuses a prospect will use to put you off and to put off buying your product or service, the most overworked and the hardest to combat from the retail salesperson's point of view is this:

"Well, I'll think it over and let you know in a few days."

Now, isn't that the truth? This is the most aggravating thing in the world to spend two hours and to talk your tonsils out trying to make a sale and then at the wind up the prospect gives you this, thanks you for your time, shakes your hand and walks away. This flabbergasts 95% of salespeople. They quit right then and there.

Here is a comeback that will pay over time for every salesperson to memorize and be courageous enough to use in such cases:

"Just a minute Mr. Jakobs, please. I appreciate that you want to think about it a little more, but I know and you know that you are better prepared right now to decide than you'll be a week from now, and here's the reason I say that. We've gone all through this thing, product features and all, even down to the financial settlement, and it's clear in your mind now to buy this product, whereas if you wait a week, other things will come up and you'll forget half the things we discussed. I believe your good judgement tells you right now to buy this product. It will take courage to do this because it is a whole lot easier to put off making a decision. It's the kind of courage that successful people have when they come to a decision, after they have looked at all the aspects of what is the right thing to do. They decide then and there. I know your best judgement is telling you right now to buy this product, and there's only one thing left to do, and that is to act, and you can do this by writing your name on this line right here." Then, hand him or her the computer, Ipad, or pencil and paper TO SIGN.

Sales have been closed by this final, desperate shot. It is so unusual that it takes the prospect by surprise and in some cases he goes right ahead and signs. At least the prospect can't help but admire your persistence and spunk, and believe me, persistence and spunk have sold many a product and service.

Now, let's consider for a moment who comes into your place to replace an outdated product they already own. He tells you he wants to upgrade to a new one. Let's say you go all out looking at his old product and then you start sobbing about what terrible shape it's in, whereupon after that he completely blows up at you about what a robber you are and then goes and buys a new one from a competitor.

How should you handle a follow up like this? In the first place, you should try to get his mind off the used product just as quickly as possible and get it on your new product. Find out what type he wants and give him a good thorough selling on it front to back, top to bottom in line with the points I have gone over. Give him a demonstration, never mentioning the old product. Don't talk about the old product at all until you have thoroughly sold the prospect on the merits of the new one. Finally, usually after the demonstration, the prospect gets "hot" and wants to know what kind of deal you are going to make with him. Take the prospect over to a desk, or if there is no desk available use the counter or a table or something—anywhere you can get away from the rabble and the lookers-on—and you can talk to the prospect privately. Make out the retail buyer's order as if the sale were already made, adding what accessories and equipment he wants, and you can sell him. Then take the total and deduct an amount—say $5 to $25—from the total price of the delivered product or service, and announce to the prospect that for so much money you will deliver him that nice new, sparkling, shiny product. Hand him the order on the laptop computer or order pad, and ask him to sign. Some prospects will ay, "Wait a minute—not so fast, what does that allow me for my old product as a trade in?"

You say, "Mr. Rogers (the manager) says that used products like this one are selling for around $____. It will need to be cleaned and shined up to sell, so the cleaning/service fee will be $____, so we can allow you $___ for it as is."

The prospect immediately blows up. "Say—you're way off! I can't **give** you my old product you know."

You tell him that you have to be fair, and that the person who buys the used product—that you wouldn't be doing him right to try to sell him a used product for more money than it is actually worth. $___ is the top price that such products are bringing on the market right now.

The prospect says he can't be bothered about the fellow whose buying his used product right now. He's got his own interests to look after.

You ask him then, "William, tell me why you are asking me to give you a discount on your new product?"

The prospect protests that he is not asking you to give him any discount on his new product and how did you get it turned around that way?

You tell him, "Yes, you are because here you say you want us to allow you $___ for a product that is worth as is only $___ and when fixed up can only be sold for $___. That means you are asking us to give us all of our commission on the deal.

Prospect says that a competitor has already offered him $___ for it and why can't you do it?

Then you ask him, "William, what kind of product would you buy if you did not have one to trade in?"

If you have sold him on your product XY Super Gadget, he will say XY Super Gadget. Sometimes he will say XY Super Gadget anyway just to be agreeable. When he does, then you can come right back at him and point out he is getting $___ worth of extra accessories on his new product, including a _____ and a _____. Add that to the extra money he is getting off the list price, and that should be sufficient to offset his argument.

However, he still maintains his old product is worth $_____, and he is going to get that much for it. You then go into detail trying to explain to him what depreciation means. Tell him that all products depreciate, and make him admit that products depreciate. Then tell him that the figures show that his used product depreciates 50% in value in the first year that it is in use, or $_____ a month. Ask him does he feel that $___ a month is fair in arriving at a depreciation figure. His product is probably two years old. $___ a month for two years is $___. Ask him how much he has used it. He'll estimate a low figure. Try to estimate the dollar value of the use he has gotten out of it so far. Ask him doesn't he think that's fair enough?

By this time the prospect should be ready to break down and cry, but maybe he's a hard customer and still holds out.

Remember the $5 to $25 I told you to hold out at the beginning of the used product discussion? Well, here's where that comes in.

Tell him, "William, I shouldn't do it, but I'll tell you what I'll do with you. I'll give you $___ for your product!"

The chances are that William will trade because he has succeeded in getting a concession out of you. You haven't lost anything because that is the figure your management gave you in the first place.

And it follows here, after all, that this kind of fellow is the kind most salespersons have to deal with all the time. Do you know who the best retail salesperson in your town is today? It is not you, your manager, or any salesperson in town. It is the person with a used product to trade.

If you can get the majority of your used products for less than the management says you can give, you are automatically a star salesperson, and if on commission, you'll make more money because of the larger cash difference. If on a salary, you are a valuable person to your employer, and they'll raise your salary. If they won't, there are other employers all over the country who are looking for valuable salespeople like you, who will. The reason they want you is the money, the $$ for a used product, is their overhead money for operations costs.

Use these strategies and you will come out a winner thanks to your eager attention to learning and practicing these sales techniques.

10

Sales Talk Starters

A quitter never wins and a winner never quits.

— Napoleon Hill

Try these sales talk conversations starters by adding your own spin:

· *At the local movie theatre this week, one man slaughtered a whole army. In our business, we slaughter whole armies of trouble in our service department.*

· *The old saying that a dog is the greatest friend a person has is very true. He will follow you to the end of the world. Our product and service will give you just as much devoted attention.*

- **How** *is it that Sam Goldstein always has money but never works. He saves his money by buying our product and services. Our product and service will save money for every Goldstein, Rodriguez, McGregor, Martinez, Fritz or any head of a family.*

- **Time** *waits for no man, but it seems to run in low to the man who has to walk to work or depend on public transportation. Our product or service will solve this problem for you.*

- **Holidays** *without a _____ are like strawberries without cream. This Fourth of July would be a real holiday if you had one of our _____ before the family celebration.*

- **We** *welcome new names, new faces, and new ideas. That is why our "Howdy" (Hello) is always working. Make us prove it. Buy a new _____.*

- ***Air*** *like a beautiful ocean is very invigorating. This is vacation season. You cannot enjoy your fishing, beach and vacation outings if you have to depend on someone else for your _____. One of our _____ will make you independent.*

- ***The*** *thing that decides a product's value is not the mere fact that it will work. How will it stand up to the daily grind? The mere fact that a mosquito can fly ten miles isn't so very interesting. But, what he does when he stops flying? He settles down to work to command your attention. These good _____ will hold up.*

- ***We*** *all believe that Santa Claus is true. We believe he brings presents to every member of the family. Our product is not in Santa Claus' line yet, but is something everyone can enjoy. Surprise your family by buying on of our _____ and make them all happy.*

- ***The*** *line between failure and success is so fine we scarcely know when we pass it. So often we are on the line and do not know it. Many a man or woman who shops for a _____ throws up his or her hands in disgust. If you wish to have success in the purchase of _____ come and see our offering at _____ this week.*

SALES TALK STARTERS

- **We** like our town, and we like our business because they are both great. There may be bigger towns that _____ but they are not better. There may be bigger companies than ours but you cannot find a better _____ than these.

- **Ancient** monarchs drove to the office in their private chariot carts. Every bump would dump the king or queen out of his or her cart. Our _____ is a vast improvement and a great method of _____.

- **The** world still needs great inventions. We need a berry box that will prevent all the best berries from staying on top. We need a golf ball with a speaker attachment which will call out "Here I am." Our _____ don't need any improvements. They speak for themselves.

- **Old** pals are the greatest thing in the world. My airplane and I crossed the ocean. My buddy and I did our military service overseas. Every piece of technology in this country did its part. If you do not have a _____ for a pal, please come on down and make a selection from our _____.

- **This** is a mistake to estimate people by some outside quality, just *the same as it is to judge a _____ by its _____. For it is that which makes the person, and it's _____ that demonstrates the quality of our _____. Our _____ will meet with your approval.*

- **Modern** *times have exploded the old saying "there is no place like home." The family who sits on the front porch and looks enviously at the neighbor who owns a _____ are vastly in the minority. There are_____ number or product owners in our country today. You can solve this family trouble if you visit our _____ department.*

- **Rah,** *rah, rah. Today and tomorrow. For football. For school. For your car. Say fellows. Let's go. Where? Down to _____ to get one of their _____.*

- **Easter** *is the time when we deck ourselves out in our new attire. We decorate our cars with new tires, new paint, new sunroofs and the purr under the hood will prove to you that the motor has had its share of attention. New clothes and one of our snappy new _____ will make this Easter complete.*

- **Perfect** *service requires a thorough understanding of your needs.*

We know our _____ will give your perfect service and at the same time will fill your needs.

- **Next** Sunday is Mother's Day. A time of glorious tribute. But, what are we going to do for Dad? Just bring him down here and help him select one of our _____. He will always remember that day.

- _____ **Company** is broadcasting our values. Tune in to channel _____. You will be sure to hear about the product or service you want. We will broadcast weekly from this station. Be sure to tune in and then come on down and see the _____. Values that cannot be duplicated. Here are some of them:_____.

- **Friday** the 13th. Maybe we can't take the jinx out of you, but we have taken the jinx out of our _____ product or service. If you don't believe it, come and see for yourself. Try one of our _____ and you will _____. Our _____ will take you where you want to go and back.

- **A** minute seems an hour when you have to get ready and go to work. Whether you have to walk, drive or you are getting bawled out for being late, or you are speeding along with your best friend. Our _____ will solve your difficult problems.

- **Transportation,** speed with the least effort is the problem that confronts the people today. Some use a bicycle, some run. Several youths have taken to flying, but anyone who wants speed with satisfaction will buy one of our _____.

- **My** wife/husband uses _____ because _(celebrity)_____ recommended it. She/he uses _____ because ____(celebrity)_____ wears them. She/he bought me a guitar when she/he saw _____celebrity) playing one. She/he should use one of _____ companies' product or service because they are the best in town.

- **No** hurry to catch an Uber or bus when you drive one of our cars. Just hurry down and look them over. Then your transportation worries will be over. How nice to be able to go where you please and come back when you are ready instead of running to catch a ride.

11

Daily Affirmations

Don't be pushed around by the fears in your mind. Be led by the dreams in your heart.

— Roy T. Bennett, The Light in the Heart

- I am a skilled salesperson.
- I am knowledgeable about the products I sell.
- I am persuasive and convincing.
- I am a great communicator.
- I am focused on developing my sales skills.
- I have a product/service that everyone wants.
- I instinctively know how to get someone to buy.
- I am in tune with my customer's needs.
- I am committed to becoming a highly successful salesperson.

- I am able to turn any transaction into one that is mutually beneficial.
- I am just naturally good at sales.
- I love making a sale.
- I am unfazed by rejection.
- Customers naturally trust and respect me.
- I have the perfect casual yet persuasive sales attitude.
- I can be convincing without being deceitful.
- My sales career is deeply satisfying.
- Demonstrating products is something I enjoy doing.
- My customers are important to me.
- I like building long term relationships with my clients.

12

In Closing

Now, to all you former, current or potential sales people out there, take this little book and use whatever pieces work for you.

You can make money selling, or you can make a ton of money selling big! In short, you can be paid to persuade.

13

Bibliography

"Albert Einstein Quotes." *BrainyQuote*, Xplore, 2020, www.brainyquote.com/quotes/albert_einstein_138243?src=t_value.

Allan, Thomas. "Sales Success Positive Affirmations." *Free Affirmations Free Positive Affirmations*, Freeaffirmations.org, 2020, www.freeaffirmations.org/sales-success-positive-affirmations.

Brudner, Emma. "75 Motivational Sales Quotes to Ignite Your Drive in 2020." *HubSpot Blog*, 2020, blog.hubspot.com/sales/motivational-quotes-sales-drive-2015.

Carnegie, Dale. *How to Win Friends and Influence People*. Diamond Pocket Books, 2019.

Hill, Napoleon, and Ross Cornwell. *Think and Grow Rich!: the Original Version, Restored and Revised*. New Holland Publishers, 2019.

Peale, Norman Vincent. *The Power of Positive Thinking ; and, The Amazing Results of Positive Thinking.* Fireside/Simon & Schuster, 2005.

14

Conclusion

Post Your Review

If you loved reading Paid to Persuade, please consider leaving me a book review by logging into your Amazon account and using the link:

www.amazon.com/review/create-review?&asin=B08KHCXDR9

Testimonial
"I have used the tried and true techniques outlined in this book to gain and close many a successful sale. The ideas are simple, down to earth and they work."
Wesley G. Harmon

Epilogue

About the Author

Diana Wolfe is a teacher and school guidance counselor who loves beaches, photography, Italian food and running around with good friends and family. She wrote this book after being inspired by the boundless energy, artful conversation, creativity and enthusiasm of her grandfather, *salesman extraordinaire and master of self-reinvention.*

About the Author

Diana Wolfe In this highly relatable, and provocative book, Diana Wolfe sets out a solid, timeless and common sense plan to double your sales income. Diana Wolfe has over twenty years experience as a corporate trainer, educator, counselor and life coach. She has a bachelor's degree in advertising and a master's degree in school guidance counseling. She lives in the greater Houston area, and loves to connect with new people. Helping people to become their best is her passion.

You can connect with me on:
🌐 https://www.goodreads.com/author/show/20248572.Diana_Wolfe

www.ingramcontent.com/pod-product-compliance
Lightning Source LLC
Chambersburg PA
CBHW031549210526
45464CB00003B/1224